IMAGES
of America

HISTORIC
CONGRESSIONAL
CEMETERY

Women sell flowers outside the Seventeenth Street gate of Historic Congressional Cemetery in 1943. (Courtesy of the Library of Congress.)

ON THE COVER: Congressional Cemetery includes 35 acres, 55,000 burial sites, and 14,000 stones. However, it is best known for its distinctive cenotaphs designed by Capitol architect Benjamin Henry Latrobe to honor members of Congress who died in office. (Courtesy of the Library of Congress.)

IMAGES
of America

HISTORIC
CONGRESSIONAL
CEMETERY

Rebecca Boggs Roberts and
Sandra K. Schmidt on behalf of the
Historic Congressional Cemetery

ARCADIA
PUBLISHING

Copyright © 2012 by Rebecca Boggs Roberts and Sandra K. Schmidt on behalf of the Historic
    Congressional Cemetery
ISBN 978-0-7385-9224-4

Published by Arcadia Publishing
Charleston, South Carolina

Printed in the United States of America

Library of Congress Control Number: 2011938566

For all general information, please contact Arcadia Publishing:
Telephone 843-853-2070
Fax 843-853-0044
E-mail sales@arcadiapublishing.com
For customer service and orders:
Toll-Free 1-888-313-2665

Visit us on the Internet at www.arcadiapublishing.com

*To the memory of the residents of the cemetery, whose
stories teach us of our rich and diverse heritage.*

—S.K.S.

*To my grandmother Lindy Boggs, who always
saw the beauty of this cemetery.*

—R.B.R.

CONTENTS

ACKNOWLEDGMENTS

Happily, the people who have devoted time and energy to saving and preserving Historic Congressional Cemetery are far too numerous to acknowledge individually. Special thanks must go to Cindy Hays, Dayle Dooley, Patrick Crowley, Terri Maxfield, Alan Davis, Elizabeth Foley, docents, dog walkers, volunteers, Steve Hammond, Linda Harper, Jim Oliver, Cindy Janke, Melvin and Thomas Mason, John Kreinheder, and Robert (Bob) Ellis, archivist at the National Archives.

The images in this volume appear courtesy of the Historic Congressional Cemetery (HCC), the Library of Congress (LOC), the District of Columbia Public Library (DCPL), the US Senate (Senate), National Portrait Gallery (NPG), and Benson J. Lossing's book *The Pictorial field-book of the War of 1812* (Lossing).

INTRODUCTION

Historic Congressional Cemetery has been a final resting place for Washingtonians for over 200 years. In 1790, when the 10-mile square along the Potomac River was chosen for a new federal district, the area was occupied by farms and plantations. The owners signed an agreement with George Washington to turn over their property for the new city, and Pierre L'Enfant mapped out a city plan by 1792. Despite elaborate planning for the new capital, no provision for burial grounds was made on any of the various city maps of the 1790s. In 1798, the commissioners of Washington set aside two squares on the borders of the city—one meant to be the eastern burial ground and one the western.

However, the eastern square was prone to flooding and was not a good choice for a cemetery. The residents of the eastern section of the city formed an association to secure a more suitable location. Most of the members of the association were also members of the Christ Church, Washington Parish vestry.

The association chose a 4.5-acre square between E and G Streets and Eighteenth and Nineteenth Streets SE. The square was purchased for $200 from the superintendent of the city. The articles of subscription, filed on April 7, 1807, stipulated that the grounds were to be laid out in three-foot-by-eight-foot sites that would be offered for sale at $2 each. The proceeds would pay for the cost of the square and for a post-and-rail fence to enclose the grounds. The articles denied burial to "infidels," and persons of color could not be interred within the area enclosed by the fence. By the terms of the articles of subscription, the graveyard would be turned over to Christ Church as soon as it was debt-free. The last debt was paid in early March 1812, and the deed and plan of the graveyard were turned over to Christ Church on March 30, 1812, when it was officially named Washington Parish Burial Ground.

The cemetery almost immediately became associated with the US Congress. In 1807, only three months after the first burial (Capitol stonecutter William Swinton), Connecticut senator Uriah Tracy died; the new cemetery was the logical place for his interment. Until the mid-1830s, practically every Congressman who died in Washington was buried in the Congressional Cemetery. In 1816, as a gesture of goodwill (and perhaps as a matter of good politics), the vestry of Christ Church set aside 100 burial sites for the interment of members of Congress—a privilege extended to their families and other government officials in 1820. Additional sites were donated to or purchased by the government, which eventually owned nearly 1,000 sites.

Over the years, the property grew to encompass 35 acres and became known as Congressional Cemetery. Christ Church still owns the property, which is administered by the nonprofit Association for the Preservation of Historic Congressional Cemetery. It is the only place in Washington where one can be buried in a site directly on L'Enfant's 18th-century city plan. If a visitor stands just inside the old iron gate at the top of the property and faces south toward the Anacostia River (while trying to ignore the jail that is visible out of the corner of a left eye), he or she can imagine it is 1807, when the cemetery was founded. The granite and marble tombstones rise on gentle slopes amid lovely brick pathways and shady old trees.

It was not always this way. For a time in the 20th century, Congressional Cemetery was forgotten and neglected. The grass grew waist high, the stones crumbled and toppled, and the back corners of the property were dirty and dangerous. By 1997, Congressional Cemetery had the dubious distinction of being added to the National Trust for Historic Preservation's list of the most endangered historic sites.

A stubborn group of dedicated Washingtonians knew the cemetery was worth saving. Local Capitol Hill neighbors who walked their dogs on the grounds began taxing themselves to pay for grass mowing. Today, the K9 Corps at Historic Congressional Cemetery has hundreds of members who pay an annual fee to walk their dogs off-leash on the grounds. Their resources and volunteer work keep the cemetery clean and secure as well as lively and well loved.

Other volunteers—including members of the armed forces, school groups, church groups, service associations, and descendant organizations—put in thousands of hours of work each year. They accomplish tasks the cemetery could never afford to pay for. Private donations, Congressional appropriations, foundation grants, and proceeds from gravesite sales have all allowed the cemetery to rebound from neglect and vandalism.

Now a National Historic Landmark, Congressional Cemetery is flourishing. The brick pathways and slate walks are restored to their original beauty. New trees are being planted and new gardens bloom. The cemetery stages regular educational events, including a reenactment of April 14, 1865, as recounted by cemetery residents who were eyewitnesses to Pres. Abraham Lincoln's last day. Other events are more festive, like a cocktail party tour of the cemetery's Prohibition-era notables, complete with a speakeasy in the public vault. School groups are regular visitors, studying everything from demography to el Día de los Muertos. Marching bands, including the world-famous US Marine Band, regularly play at the grave of John Philip Sousa. Genealogists, photographers, historians, dog walkers, birders, joggers, anthropologists, and Victorian scholars can all find something to love among the old stones. And as an active cemetery, Congressional boasts some new stones, too, many of which are creative and surprising.

Congressional Cemetery has seen the federal district along the Potomac River grow into a busy modern city. Washington, DC, now fills 61 square miles with 600,000 residents. The block that was deemed too wet to be the eastern burial ground in 1798 is now the heart of the revitalized Atlas District. Over 55,000 people have been buried at Congressional Cemetery, and infidels and persons of color are now welcome. As it enters its third century, the history of the city—and, indeed, the United States—will continue to be written on the stones of Congressional Cemetery.

One

THE WASHINGTON PARISH BURIAL GROUND

A NEW CEMETERY IN A NEW CITY

In the early 19th century, the "rural" cemetery movement gained popularity in the United States. Instead of flat, square churchyards, cemeteries became sylvan parks with landscaped paths and serene vistas. The cemetery functioned as a public park; many tombstones in Congressional Cemetery are shaped like tables, and families would visit for the day and bring a picnic lunch to eat at the grave. (HCC.)

Christ Church, Washington Parish, G Street, between Sixth and Seventh Sts., S. E.

Of the eight men charged with finding an appropriate site for a burial ground on the eastern side of the city, most of them were members of the vestry of Christ Church, Washington Parish, the oldest Episcopal Church on Capitol Hill. When the original 4.5 acres of cemetery property were purchased in 1807, the articles of subscription specified that the graveyard would be turned over to Christ Church as soon as it was debt-free. The new cemetery was called Washington Parish Burial Ground and was signed over to Christ Church in 1812—debt-free after just five years in business. Christ Church still owns the cemetery property, but it is administered by the nonprofit Association for the Preservation of Historic Congressional Cemetery. (DCPL.)

On April 11, 1807, just days after the land was purchased, William Swinton was the first person buried at the new cemetery. Swinton was a stonecutter who had been recruited by architect Benjamin Henry Latrobe to help build the nearby US Capitol. His grave is marked with a thin sandstone tablet engraved with colonial calligraphy, a style that fell out of fashion only a few years later. The handful of other stones in that style are all among the earliest graves on the property. (Both, HCC.)

Another early burial at the Washington Parish Burial Ground was Margaret Tingey, who died in April 1807. Margaret was the wife of Commodore Thomas Tingey, a member of the Christ Church vestry and a founder of the cemetery. As commandant of the nearby Navy Yard, Commodore Tingey achieved some fame in the War of 1812. In August 1814, invading British soldiers marched on Washington, bent on destruction. Tingey, not wanting the young United States' naval assets to fall into the hands of the enemy, gave the order to torch the Navy Yard. The fire was reportedly lit by Mordecai Booth, who is buried near the Tingey plot. (HCC.)

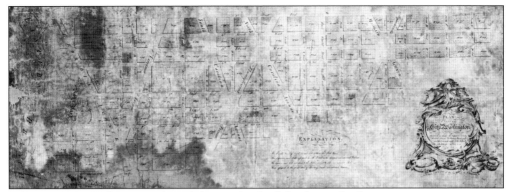

When George Washington selected the site for the federal city, the first priority was to negotiate with the 10 men who owned and farmed the land. One of the landowners was William Prout, whose holdings included much of Capitol Hill and southeast Washington from the Capitol to the Navy Yard. As the owner of such prime real estate, Prout received a personal invitation from President Washington to come to Washington to negotiate terms for selling part of his land to the government. He was flattered by Washington's attention and willingly signed the agreement between the government and the other landowners. (Above, LOC; below, HCC.)

Building the federal city demanded a large workforce of skilled craftsmen and laborers, but there was little in the way of housing and comforts to attract workmen to the city. Recruiters roamed far and wide—including to England, Scotland, and Germany—in search of skilled workers. Many of those who agreed to come to the city stayed and are interred in Congressional Cemetery. Stonemason George Blagden was born in Yorkshire, England, but was living in Philadelphia when he accepted the position of overseer of construction at the Capitol. He held the position from 1793 until his death in 1826 as a result of a trench that caved in while he was inspecting the foundations of the Capitol. He was also among the founders of Congressional Cemetery. (HCC.)

In 1793, at the age of 28, James Greenleaf was appointed US consul in Holland, where he met and married a Dutch baroness. He reputedly amassed a fortune exceeding $1 million—a fabulous sum in those days—and fully expected to make another fortune investing in property in the new federal city. His first and largest purchase was 3,000 lots in what was originally called Turkey Buzzard Point (renamed Greenleaf's Point and now called Fort McNair). He eventually acquired 6,000 lots and promised to build at least 10 houses per year; over the years, he constructed some of the city's most famous residences. Greenleaf's ambitions were thwarted when the Napoleonic Wars deprived him of expected financial support from Dutch colleagues. To make matters worse, lot sales in Washington never met expectations, and the appreciation of land values was sluggish. Although he eventually went bankrupt, Greenleaf avoided debtors' prison and lived to a comfortable old age in the city that his financial dealings nearly destroyed. (HCC.)

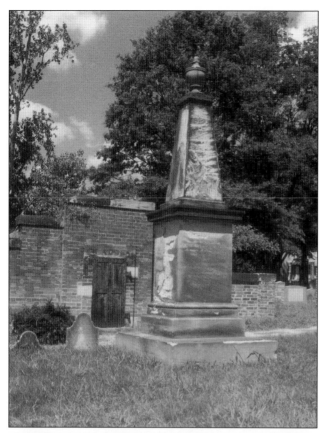

Another cemetery founder, Samuel Smallwood, went on to become both the fifth and seventh mayor of the District of Columbia. He began his working life as the overseer of slaves at the Capitol construction site and eventually became a wealthy lumber dealer. Smallwood had begun his second term as mayor when he suddenly died. His last act created the committee to make arrangements to receive and entertain Marquis de Lafayette, the general of Revolutionary War fame. Several small graves of Smallwood infants are next to the large Smallwood family monument. (Both, HCC.)

As the cemetery grew, so did its prestige. Wealthy Washington families bought several burial sites, built grand monuments, and erected stone coping or iron fences around the edges of the plot emblazoned with the family name. William Gunton was president of the Bank of Washington, and Edward Temple was his son-in-law. Temple took over as bank president when Gunton died. Mary Jane Gunton Temple built the Gunton-Temple Memorial Church in honor of her husband and father, which stood at Fourteenth and R Streets until it was razed in 1922. At least 12 Guntons and Temples from several generations are buried in the family plot. (DCPL.)

Washington Parish Burial Ground was the first de facto national cemetery and the burial place for many veterans before the national cemetery system began during the Civil War. The cemetery is full of military stones—for veterans who fought in American wars from the revolution to the 21st century—only distinguishable by the dates. One exception is found among the stones for Civil War veterans who fought for the Confederacy; their stones have pointed tops—legend has it so that no "damn Yankee" would sit on them. (Both, HCC.)

One way the cemetery grew was by accepting reburials from other cemeteries that were being redeveloped. Baron J.P.C. De Krafft was a German dignitary who served during the Revolutionary War and was known for the accuracy of his cartography. When he died in 1804, he was buried in the Presbyterian Cemetery in Georgetown. De Krafft was reinterred when Presbyterian closed, and his stone was moved along with his remains, which explains why the stone is older than the cemetery. Congressional Cemetery is the final resting place of many of De Krafft's descendants. (Both, HCC.)

It was not long before the cemetery became the fashionable place to spend eternity. Those with the means built family vaults or mausoleums. Most vaults are built into the earth and reached through a set of steep stairs. These mausoleums are entirely aboveground. Similar imposing granite structures are found throughout the cemetery and generally stand alone. This row of family vaults faces south near the southern edge of the cemetery. Behind their ornate iron gates are stacks of burial niches. As each niche was filled, it was sealed with a marble plaque engraved with the name of the deceased. Some families outgrew their first structure and built a second mausoleum in the same row. (LOC.)

In keeping with the rural cemetery tradition, visitors were encouraged to use the cemetery as a park. The paths were lined with shady trees, and a decorative fountain was installed at a high point near the center of the property in 1869. (DCPL.)

The fountain was replaced by a chapel in 1903. At the time, the chapel was considered a state-of-the-art structure with six ventilated coffin bays and plenty of seating. The chapel has been entirely restored and reconsecrated and now serves as a place not just for funerals, but also for weddings, lectures, meetings, book signings, and receptions. (LOC.)

Eventually, an ornate iron fence was built to enclose the property. A house was built at the front gate for the cemetery manager and his family. The house was topped with a bell tower, and one of the cemetery manager's jobs was to toll the bell during a funeral. This house was replaced with the current one in 1923, but the bell still exists and is still tolled for funerals and other commemorative occasions. (DCPL.)

Two

THE CONGRESSIONAL
CEMETERY
A NATIONAL FINAL RESTING PLACE

Although the cemetery's official name was Washington Parish Burial Ground, it was locally known as Congressional Cemetery almost from the beginning. The cemetery owners at Christ Church, Washington Parish, recognizing a productive relationship when they saw one, encouraged the nickname. The name was set in iron when a new front gate was built, along with a new manager's house, in 1923. (HCC.)

The first member of Congress to be buried at the cemetery was Sen. Uriah Tracy of Connecticut, who died in office just a few months after the cemetery opened in 1807. Embalming was uncommon before the Civil War, and the limited options for transporting Tracy's body back to Connecticut were slow and unreliable. It immediately became clear that the new cemetery was the most appropriate place for his burial. Benjamin Henry Latrobe, the architect of the Capitol building, was asked to design a Congressional monument to mark Tracy's grave—and those of other members of Congress who would follow. (LOC.)

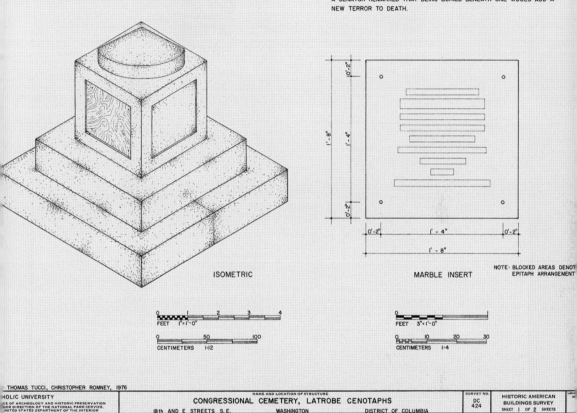

CONGRESSIONAL CEMETERY
LATROBE CENOTAPHS

THESE CENOTAPHS WERE DESIGNED BY NOTED ARCHITECT BENJAMIN HENRY LATROBE IN 1815 AS MEMORIALS TO CONGRESSMEN WHO DIED IN OFFICE. ALTHOUGH SEVERAL HUNDRED OF THE MONUMENTS WERE ERECTED, LESS THAN EIGHTY BODIES OF CONGRESSMEN AND PROMINENT CITIZENS WERE INTERRED UNDER THEM. THEIR USE WAS DISCONTINUED IN 1877 AFTER A SENATOR REMARKED THAT BEING BURIED BENEATH ONE WOULD ADD A NEW TERROR TO DEATH.

ISOMETRIC

MARBLE INSERT

NOTE: BLOCKED AREAS DENOT EPITAPH ARRANGEMENT

0 1 2 3 4
FEET   1"=1'-0"

0   50   100
CENTIMETERS   1:12

0   10   20   30
FEET   3"=1'-0"

0   10   20   30
CENTIMETERS   1:4

THOMAS TUCCI, CHRISTOPHER ROMNEY, 1976

HOLIC UNIVERSITY
CE OF ARCHEOLOGY AND HISTORIC PRESERVATION
DER DIRECTION OF THE NATIONAL PARK SERVICE,
UNITED STATES DEPARTMENT OF THE INTERIOR

NAME AND LOCATION OF STRUCTURE
CONGRESSIONAL CEMETERY, LATROBE CENOTAPHS
18th AND E STREETS S.E.   WASHINGTON   DISTRICT OF COLUMBIA

SURVEY NO.
DC
424

HISTORIC AMERICAN
BUILDINGS SURVEY
SHEET 1 OF 2 SHEETS

Latrobe designed his monument to be easily hewn and installed. It was to be made from the same Aquia Creek sandstone as the Capitol itself. The cube shape with the small dome on top echoes the classical architecture of the Capitol and other federal buildings. Latrobe specifically wanted a heavy, wide monument—he felt the traditional tablets of the day did not last long enough to honor the memory of members of the US Congress. (LOC.)

As transportation improved, the families of deceased members of Congress chose to bury them back in their home districts. The markers were placed in Congressional Cemetery anyway, starting the tradition of installing Latrobe's monuments for any member of Congress who died in office—regardless of whether he was actually buried at Congressional Cemetery. This tradition

continued until 1877. The stones became known as "cenotaphs," which means empty tombs. There are 171 of them in the cemetery, but the remains of only 59 congressmen rest beneath them; there is no way to tell from a stone whether the grave beneath is occupied or empty. (LOC.)

The cenotaphs are uniform, installed in neat rows, and, as author Frances Trollope sniffed in 1827, "without any pretension to splendor." Even former president John Quincy Adams got no special attention. Adams, elected to the House of Representatives after his term as president, died in the US Capitol in 1848. His body is interred in Massachusetts; his marker in Congressional Cemetery is a true cenotaph. (HCC.)

There is one exception to the uniformity of the sandstone cenotaphs. Although it is the same shape as the other Congressional markers, the stone for William Upham is fashioned from rough-hewn gray granite. Senator Upham, a noted abolitionist, represented the state of Vermont, and his cenotaph showcases local Vermont stone. (Above, HCC; right, LOC.)

William Thornton was not a member of Congress—he was a medical doctor who won the public contest to design the US Capitol building in 1793. His prize was $500 and a lot in the new federal city. Thornton went on to hold several federal positions in Washington, including head of the patent office in the James Madison administration. In those days, the patent office included tiny models of American inventions. When the invading British threatened to burn the patent office in 1814, Thornton successfully convinced them the loss would be a blow to all mankind, not just Americans. In recognition of his association with the Capitol building, Thornton's grave is marked with a Latrobe monument—one of only three that mark the grave of a civilian. (Above, HCC; below, LOC.)

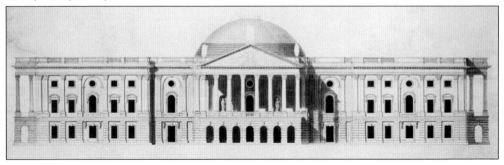

John C. Calhoun (left cenotaph) was a senator from South Carolina when he died in 1850. Famous for his fiery speeches and staunch defense of slavery, Calhoun was an inspiration for southern secessionists years after his death. Henry Clay (right cenotaph), the senator from Kentucky, was known as "the Great Compromiser" for his ability to bring enemy factions into agreement. In life, the two men loathed each other, but the timing of their deaths led their cenotaphs to be placed side by side for eternity. The tradition of installing Congressional cenotaphs ended in 1877. Because of advances in embalming and the acceleration of the national cemetery system after the Civil War, most members of Congress were sent home for burial. Also, the monuments were considered ugly. Sen. George Frisbie Hoar, of Massachusetts, stated that the idea of being buried under one "brings a new horror to death." (HCC.)

By 1835, so many public burial processions were taking place at the cemetery that Congress agreed to build a public vault. Built for $5,000, the vault was intended as a temporary holding place for bodies while funeral arrangements were being made. There was no charge for a member of Congress to use the vault; others paid $5 per month. Most bodies only stayed for a day or two, including those of Vice Pres. John C. Calhoun and Presidents John Quincy Adams, William Henry Harrison, and Zachary Taylor. One notable exception was the body of First Lady Dolley Madison, which remained in the public vault for two years after her death in 1849; James Causten, the father-in-law of Dolley's niece, removed her to his family vault across the pathway. She remained there until the Causten family had her reinterred at Montpelier in 1858. The remains of over 3,000 people were held in the public vault over the years; the vault fell out of regular use in the 1930s. (LOC.)

In 2005, the public vault was repaired and restored. No longer a holding place for remains, it is now a popular stop on cemetery tours. It is also put to good use at cemetery events. Like the family vaults nearby, only the top third of the vault is visible from street level—the rest is subterranean, reached by a steep set of steps down into the earth. (HCC.)

Although the tradition of installing Congressional monuments was discontinued in 1877, there is one cenotaph of recent vintage. Hale Boggs was a congressman from Louisiana and majority leader of the House when he traveled to Alaska in 1972 to campaign for Congressman Nicholas Begich. The small plane they were traveling in disappeared, and no wreckage or remains were ever found. A cenotaph was installed in their honor in 1981. Boggs's name is on one side; Begich's is on the other. Set slightly apart from the historic stones, this cenotaph is indistinguishable from those that are a century and a half older. (Both, HCC.)

A member of the House of Representatives for 34 years, Thomas P. "Tip" O'Neill was Speaker of the House when he attended the dedication of the cenotaph for Representatives Hale Boggs and Nicholas Begich. Charmed by the tradition, O'Neill wanted his own marker in Congressional Cemetery, although his is of more contemporary design. O'Neill's stone is a cenotaph; he is buried in Boston. (HCC.)

VIEW AT THE CONGRESSIONAL CEMETERY
WASHINGTON, D.C.

Publ. at the Music Depot of W. G. Metzerott.

Despite their reputation for homeliness, the Latrobe cenotaphs are a distinctive feature of Congressional Cemetery. This Victorian postcard somewhat over romanticizes the lushness of the cemetery foliage, but the cenotaphs are instantly recognizable. The cenotaphs are unique to Congressional and have been for over 200 years, no matter their aesthetic merits. (DCPL.)

Three

FAMOUS RESIDENTS
THE MARCH KING, THE DIRECTOR, THE CHIEF, AND MORE

By the middle of the 19th century, Congressional Cemetery was a prestigious place to spend eternity. Grand funerals for federal dignitaries stretched for miles down Pennsylvania Avenue, and ornate horse-drawn hearses, as seen in this 1913 photograph, carried the honored dead to the cemetery chapel. However, many of the best-known cemetery residents are not at Congressional because of their national prominence, but because they were Washingtonians who grew up on Capitol Hill. (DCPL.)

John Philip Sousa grew up just blocks away from Congressional Cemetery, near the Marine barracks on Eighth Street SE. Sousa played several instruments as a child (his father was also a musician and is buried nearby), and family legend has it that he threatened to run off with a circus band as a teenager. His father enlisted him in the Marines instead. Sousa became leader of the Marine band in 1880 and wrote dozens of compositions for the band to play. (Above, HCC; left, LOC.)

The popularity of compositions like "The Stars and Stripes Forever," "Semper Fidelis," and "The Washington Post" march earned Sousa the nickname "The March King." His large family grave includes his wife and children, as well as a commemorative bench. The grave is a popular spot for visiting marching bands from across America, who often stop at the cemetery to play a Sousa tune or two while in Washington, DC. The US Marine Band visits the March King and pays tribute to him every year on his birthday, November 6. (Both, HCC.)

J. Edgar Hoover was a third-generation Washingtonian who grew up near Eastern Market on Seward Square SE. His father, Dickerson Hoover, bought a plot in Congressional Cemetery in 1893 upon the death of his three-year-old daughter Sadie. As a young Justice Department agent, J. Edgar Hoover made a name for himself navigating the tricky politics of Prohibition-era Washington. As the first director of the Federal Bureau of Investigation (FBI), Hoover is credited with making that agency the powerful force it became. (Above, HCC; below, LOC.)

J. Edgar Hoover never married and was buried with his parents and sister when he died in 1972. The decorative iron fence, featuring the FBI seal, was installed by a retired FBI agent in 1996. New FBI recruits still come to visit Hoover when they join the bureau. The gravesite contains an iron bench with the FBI seal—also a gift from former agents. (HCC.)

Originally a teacher and school administrator, Belva Lockwood moved to Washington in 1865 and became active in the fight for equal rights for women. Lockwood lobbied for a bill that would give federal female employees the same salaries as their male counterparts. A widow with one young daughter, Lockwood attended the National University Law School (now the George Washington University Law School). She was not allowed to study with the men and was denied her diploma until she personally petitioned Pres. Ulysses S. Grant to give her what she had earned. (Both, LOC.)

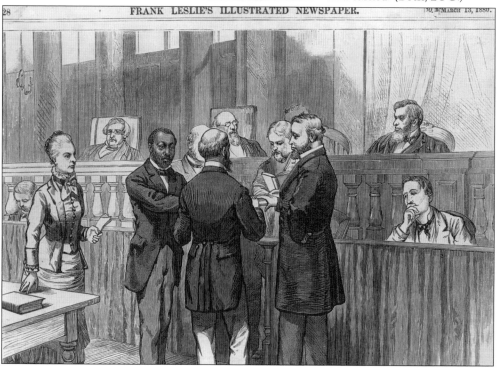

FRANK LESLIE'S ILLUSTRATED NEWSPAPER.

In 1879, Lockwood lobbied for and became the first woman to argue before the Supreme Court. Perhaps her most significant victory was winning a $5 million settlement for the Cherokee in compensation for their forced removal. In 1884, Lockwood became the first woman to run for president on a major party ticket as the nominee of the Equal Rights party, although she, herself, could not vote. An ardent worker for women's suffrage, she died in 1917, three years before women were granted the right to vote in the United States. (Right, HCC; below, LOC.)

Mathew Brady is known as the father of photojournalism. His images of the Civil War included not only heroic portraits of soldiers and generals, but more candid scenes of encampments and battles. Widely published in newspapers, Brady's images of war showed Americans what was going on at the front in vivid detail. His portrait of Abraham Lincoln is the source for the image on the $5 bill. (Both, LOC.)

Brady's Incidents of the War

Mathew Brady hoped to sell his photographic collection to the federal government as an archival record of the Civil War. At the time, the government was not interested, and by the end of his life Brady was almost destitute. He was also blind as a result of exposure to darkroom chemicals and could no longer take photographs. He is buried in the family plot of his wife, Julia Handy Brady. His nephew Levin Handy, also a noted photographer, inherited the photograph collection. In 1954, the Library of Congress purchased the collection of over 10,000 photographs from Levin Handy's daughters. (Above, HCC; below, LOC.)

Elbridge Gerry came to Washington in 1812 as James Madison's second vice president. He died in office in 1814 and was buried at Congressional Cemetery. His grave is marked by an imposing monument topped with a marble eternal flame and includes Gerry's own words as his epitaph, "It is the duty of every citizen, though he may have but one day to live, to devote that day to the good of his country." It is visited every Fourth of July by patriotic organizations like the Sons of the American Revolution. (LOC.)

Elbridge Gerry is the only signer of the Declaration of Independence who is buried in the Washington, DC, area. Gerry attended the Continental Congresses as a representative from Massachusetts, where his family included prominent merchants. Gerry became governor of Massachusetts in 1810. In 1812, he signed a redistricting bill that included an oddly shaped Congressional district. The local press said it looked like a mythical animal and called it a "gerrymander." The name (and the practice of drawing odd districts) endures. (Both, LOC.)

Gen. Alexander Macomb was born in Detroit to a merchant family. Macomb joined a New York militia company at age 16, advancing to first lieutenant in the Corps of Engineers, the newly created unit that constituted the US military academy at the time. He was one of the first officers to complete training at West Point, later becoming chief engineer in charge of coastal fortifications in the Carolinas and Georgia. In the War of 1812, as a brigadier general, he defeated the British at Plattsburg, New York, though outnumbered 10 to 1, and was signally honored by Congress and made brevet major general. In 1821, he came to Washington as head of the Corps of Engineers and was designated commanding general of the US Army in 1828. (Left, HCC; below, LOC.)

MAJOR GEN! A. MACOMB.

Printed by Pendleton, Kearny & Childs, Philadelphia.

MACOMB'S MONUMENT.

Macomb's monument, topped by an impressive Corinthian helmet, has been a popular cemetery attraction since Macomb's death in 1841. By 2007, however, it was noticeably listing to one side. When the National Park Service came to the cemetery to right it, they discovered the monument was actually a crypt; there was a brick vault below the stone that contained the remains of Macomb and his wife, Catherine. (Lossing.)

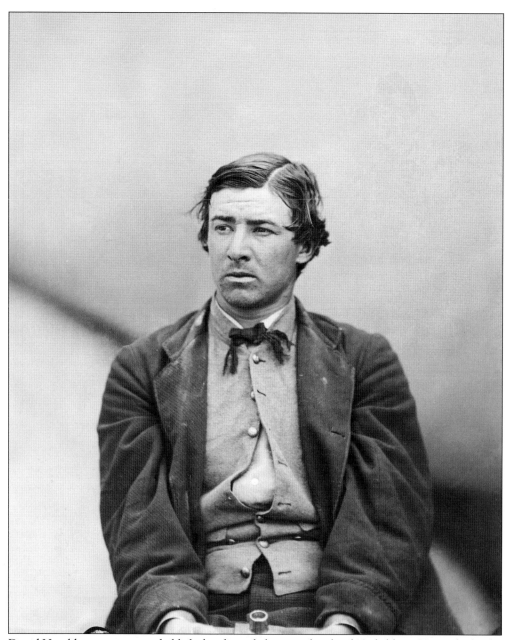

David Herold was an unremarkable kid—the only boy in a family of 10 children. He studied to be a pharmacist but never really amounted to much in his profession. Through his school friend John Surratt, he met John Wilkes Booth and joined an elaborate conspiracy that originally intended to kidnap Pres. Abraham Lincoln and ransom him for Confederate prisoners. After Robert E. Lee surrendered at Appomattox, the plot became more deadly, targeting not only the president, but also the vice president and secretary of state. Herold's job was to help the murderers get away, since he knew his way around the Maryland countryside. (LOC.)

On April 14, 1865, John Wilkes Booth shot and killed President Lincoln. The other assassination attempts failed, but Herold met up with Booth and helped keep him on the run for 12 days. When Union soldiers caught up with the fugitives, Booth was shot and Herold gave himself up. Herold was hanged alongside coconspirators George Atzerodt, Lewis Powell, and Mary Surratt. He was buried near the gallows at what is now Fort McNair. (LOC.)

In 1869, the pastor of St. John's Episcopal Church petitioned President Johnson, on behalf of Herold's mother and sisters, to have his body moved to the family plot at Congressional Cemetery. The petition was approved, but no tombstone was placed on the site for fear of vandalism. His sister Elizabeth was interred in the same site when she died in 1903. (HCC.)

Leonard Matlovich, an Air Force veteran of the Vietnam War, was awarded the Bronze Star for his service. When he told his commanding officer he was gay, Matlovich was discharged. He became a gay rights activist, with particular emphasis on the rights of gays in the military. He designed his own gravestone from the same reflective black granite as the Vietnam Veterans Memorial Wall. His provocative epitaph reads "When I was in the military they gave me a medal for killing two men—and a discharge for loving one." His grave continues to be a rallying place for gay rights activists, particularly gay veterans. (Both, HCC.)

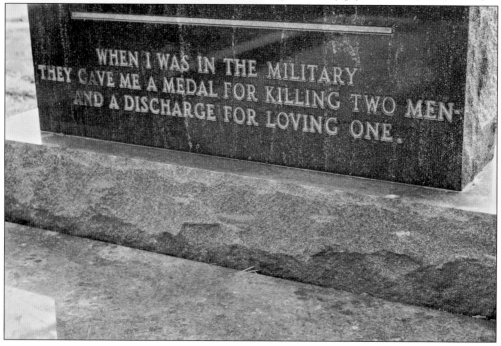

Two large and ornate statues mark the gravesites of the Hall family. Mary Ann Hall and her sister are buried under the contemplative maiden on the right, and Mary's mother and her other sister are buried under the angel. Hall was not bold enough to mark her own grave with an angel, since her wealth was derived from the business that she ran—the fanciest bordello in Civil War–era Washington. Her house stood at the corner of Maryland and Independence Avenues, literally in the shadow of the Capitol. When the National Museum of the American Indian was designed for the site in 1997, an environmental impact assessment team found the bordello's trash pit—it was full of shards of fine porcelain and Piper-Heidsieck champagne corks. (HCC.)

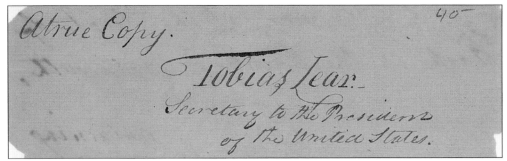

Tobias Lear began his professional life as George Washington's private secretary. He was at Mount Vernon when Washington died, and it fell to Lear to arrange the funeral. Lear was also responsible for being the curator of Washington's papers and was blamed for the disappearance of a few potentially controversial pieces of correspondence with Thomas Jefferson. (LOC.)

After Washington's death, President Jefferson assigned Lear diplomatic posts, none of which were particularly successful. Lear died by his own hand in 1816. The epitaph on his marble-covered box tomb has almost completely eroded, leaving only the final line legible: "City of Silence." (HCC.)

Some call Push-ma-ta-ha the greatest Choctaw chief who ever lived. While other American Indian tribes sided with the British in the War of 1812, Push-ma-ta-ha led the Choctaw in alliance with the Americans. Andrew Jackson credited his 500 Choctaw soldiers with ensuring an American victory at the Battle of New Orleans. In 1824, when Jackson was a senator, Push-ma-ta-ha came to Washington to remind Jackson of their alliance and ask the federal government to honor the treaties signed during the war. While in Washington, Push-ma-ta-ha caught a fatal fever. Among his final words was the request that "the big guns be fired over me." That wish was granted in an elaborate funeral ceremony and miles-long procession. The words are carved on Push-ma-ta-ha's gravestone, the shape of which echoes the Congressional markers nearby. (Right, LOC; below, HCC.)

Born in Charleston, South Carolina, Robert Mills, pictured above with his wife, Eliza, is sometimes called the first native-born American architect. He designed buildings throughout the mid-Atlantic states, influenced by Neoclassical ideals. His works include the Sansom Street Baptist Church in Philadelphia, the first American church with a domed roof. He came to Washington as the architect of public buildings and designed the old Treasury Building, the old US Post Office, and the old Patent Office (now the Donald W. Reynolds Center for American Art and Portraiture). (LOC.)

In 1836, Robert Mills designed his most famous structure, the Washington Monument. His original design was substantially altered, however, and the simple obelisk that stands today was not completed until years after Mills's death in 1855. Ironically (for a man who designed monuments), Mills's own grave went unmarked until 1936, when the American Institute of Architects installed the current stone. (Right, LOC; below, HCC.)

Joseph Gales moved to Washington around 1807 to join the *National Intelligencer* newspaper. A few years later, he and his brother-in-law William Seaton became the owners of the paper. The paper was vehemently anti-British. When British troops marched on Washington in 1814, they were under orders to only destroy public buildings and spare private property—they made an exception for the offices of the *Intelligencer*. Gales had published articles criticizing the admiral, and legend has it that British admiral George Cockburn personally smashed every "C" in the printing press before setting the building on fire so the newspaper could no longer print his name. The paper was back up and running the next day. (Left, Senate; below, HCC.)

Henry Schoolcraft was an explorer, ethnographer, and naturalist. While exploring the Midwest as a geologist and mineralogist for the federal government, Schoolcraft decided to study American Indian tribes and introduce their cultures to others. He joined the 1820 Cass Expedition to the Lake Superior copper region. He made further expeditions throughout the Midwest and is credited with discovering the source of the Mississippi River in the early 1830s. Schoolcraft's wide acquaintance with the Indians led to his appointment as Indian agent for the tribes of Lake Superior, and his collection of Native American tales was the basis for Henry Wadsworth Longfellow's poem, *The Song of Hiawatha*. (Right, LOC; below, HCC.)

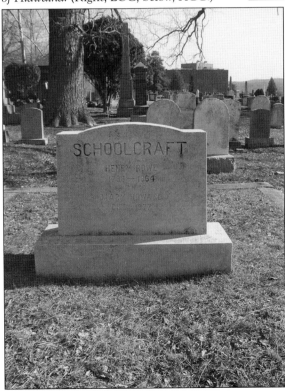

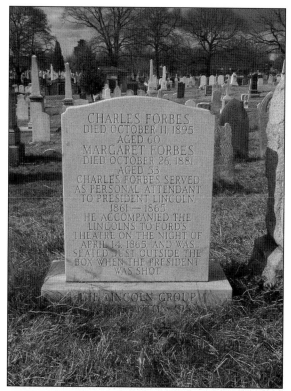

Charles Forbes was Pres. Abraham Lincoln's valet. On April 14, 1865, Forbes accompanied the president and first lady to Ford's Theatre, stopping on the way to pick up their guests, Henry Rathbone and Clara Harris. In the age before the president had personal protection from the Secret Service, it was Forbes who sat outside the president's box at the theater, and it was Forbes who told John Wilkes Booth, a handsome and well-known actor, that he was welcome to enter the box and pay the president his respects. Forbes regretted granting that permission until the day he died in 1895. (Left, HCC; below, LOC.)

ASSASSINATION OF PRESIDENT LINCOLN,

AT FORD'S THEATRE APL. 14TH 1865.

"TREASON AND MURDER WORK TOGETHER."

Published by H.H.Lloyd & Cº 21 John St New York.

Born in France, Joseph Nicollet grew to eminence as a mathematician and astronomer. He was particularly distinguished as an observer of physical astronomy. Nicollet authored several significant works, including papers and memoirs in astronomy and the higher mathematics, which gave him an enviable reputation in the scientific world. He emigrated to America in 1829 and, after traveling for a few years, was engaged by the secretary of war to make a scientific exploration of the vast regions beyond the Mississippi and Missouri Rivers. He mapped the headwaters of the Mississippi, paying careful attention to the history, laws, customs, and language of the Indian tribes, collecting vocabulary and grammar of numerous dialects. A Minnesota county, a town, and Nicollet Avenue in Minneapolis are named in his honor. (Right, HCC; below, LOC.)

As a judge in California in the 1850s, Henry Worthington fought seven duels to defend his pro-Union views, winning all of them and leaving six fatalities behind. During the Civil War, he moved to Nevada, becoming that state's first congressman in 1864. Worthington held a few diplomatic posts and died in Washington in 1909. He was the last surviving pallbearer of Abraham Lincoln. His grave at Congressional Cemetery was marked with a modest nameplate until 2000, when some prominent Nevadans installed a larger stone engraved with the state flag. (HCC.)

When the Cherokee who survived the Trail of Tears settled in the new Indian Territory in 1839, it was William Shorey Coodey who drafted the Cherokee Constitution, uniting the former nations of Eastern and Western Cherokee. In the early 1840s, a new combined Cherokee government began to function with William Shorey Coodey as president of the senate. As such, he was acting principal chief in 1846 during the absence of both the principal chief and the assistant principal chief. (HCC.)

William Wirt was a lawyer who practiced in Virginia and Maryland and first rose to prominence in the 1807 prosecution of Aaron Burr for treason. Wirt's four-hour speech became famous for its wit and eloquence. Wirt became Pres. James Monroe's attorney general in 1817 and retained his post under Pres. John Quincy Adams. As the longest-serving attorney general in US history, he is credited with making the position the prominent job it is today. Wirt's monument, the largest in Congressional Cemetery, sits on top of a family crypt. The crypt was vandalized some time in the 20th century, and Wirt's skull was stolen. It was returned and reinterred in 2005. (Right, NPG; below, DCPL.)

Adelaide Johnson was an artist, a suffragist, and an eccentric best known for *Portrait Monument*, the statue of Elizabeth Cady Stanton, Susan B. Anthony, and Lucretia Mott. It was presented by the National Woman's Party as a gift to the nation on February 15, 1921, and placed in the Rotunda Hall of the Capitol. However, it was swiftly moved to the Capitol Crypt; detractors and critics derisively nicknamed it "Three Women in a Bathtub." Finally, after 76 years, a Congressional resolution provided for the sculpture's move back to the Rotunda over Mother's Day weekend in May 1997. (LOC.)

Drama seemed to follow Adelaide Johnson. In her 20s, she slipped down an elevator shaft and was awarded enough money to give her some measure of financial freedom—rare for a single woman in the late 19th century. In 1896, she married Alexander Jenkins, a man 12 years her junior; he took her name as "the tribute love pays to genius." Her bridesmaids were the busts she had sculpted of Susan B. Anthony and Elizabeth Cady Stanton. Perennially in debt, Johnson did everything she could to raise funds, including appearing on the game show *Strike It Rich*. She also threw herself a 100th birthday party when she was only 88. Some of the cemetery records indicate she was 108 at death, though she was (only) 96. (Right, HCC; below, LOC.)

.LAYING CORNER STONE WASHINGTON MONUMENT.

As Grand Master of the DC Masonic Lodge, Benjamin B. French laid the cornerstone of the Washington Monument in 1848. French was appointed commissioner of public buildings under Pres. Franklin Pierce and again under President Lincoln's administration, a position he held throughout the Civil War. French also kept detailed diaries, often used as a primary source for descriptions of Civil War–era Washington. (Left, LOC; below, HCC.)

Archibald Henderson served on the USS *Constitution* during the War of 1812. In 1820, at the age of 37, he was appointed the fifth commandant of the Marine Corps, a responsibility he held until his death almost 39 years later. During his tenure in office, Henderson saw the corps through a host of small campaigns and seaborne operations and personally led a Marine regiment in the early campaigns of the Seminole War. He is well known for having left a note pinned to his door that said, "Gone to Florida to fight the Indians. Will be back when the war is over." He commanded the corps during the Mexican War, and by the time of his death—on the eve of the Civil War—had insured the continued role of his beloved Marine Corps as a strong force in the American military. Marine lore has it that at a party in Maj. Gen. Commandant Thomas Holcomb's house in 1942, General Henderson's portrait fell from the wall when Holcomb voiced his decision to recruit women into the Marine Corps. (Right, HCC; below, LOC.)

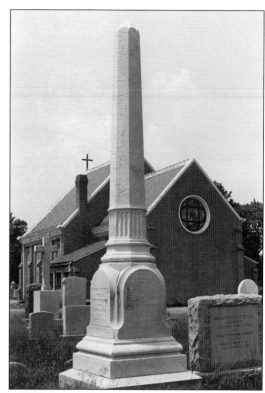

GENERAL BROWN'S MONUMENT.

In 1800, Jacob Brown took up farming on the shore of Lake Ontario, founding the town of Brownville. He became active in the state militia and took command of the New York frontier at the outbreak of the War of 1812. After successfully repelling British attacks at Ogdensburg and Sackets Harbor, he rose to the rank of brigadier general in 1813. At the battle of Lundy's Lane, Brown was badly wounded and was forced to retire, giving up his ultimate objective, the capture of York (now Toronto). Brown became senior officer of the Army in June 1815 and was appointed to the newly created post of commanding general in June 1821, a post he held until his death. His monument, a broken column, is meant to represent life cut short. (Above left, HCC; above right, HCC; below right, LOC.)

Anne Royall, by some accounts the first professional female journalist in the United States, grew up in the mountains of western Virginia. There, she met and married Maj. William Royall. Upon William's death, his children contested his will, leaving Anne Royall almost penniless. She came to Washington in 1824 to petition for a federal pension as the widow of a veteran, which at that time had to be done in person. She started a newspaper called the *Huntress* (and later *Paul Pry*) and became known for her exposes of corruption and cronyism. Legend has it that Royall once caught Pres. John Quincy Adams during his early morning bath in the Potomac River. The enterprising Royall gathered the president's clothes and sat on them until he answered her questions, earning her the first presidential interview ever granted to a woman. (Both, HCC.)

CLINTON'S TOMB.

George Clinton was a delegate to the Continental Congress from New York in 1775, but he never signed the Declaration of Independence because he obeyed George Washington's orders to take to the revolutionary battlefields as brigadier general of militia. Clinton was governor of New York during the American Revolution, and serving as a wartime governor made Clinton very nervous about a powerful federal government. When New York held its constitutional ratification convention in 1788, Clinton was one of the most vocal opponents of the new Constitution. Clinton served as New York's governor for seven terms—still a record in the state. In 1804, Thomas Jefferson chose Clinton to replace Aaron Burr as his vice president. Clinton also served as vice president in the first Madison administration. He died in office in 1812 and was buried in Congressional Cemetery. In 1908, his remains and monument were moved to Kingston, New York. (Left, Lossing; below, LOC.)

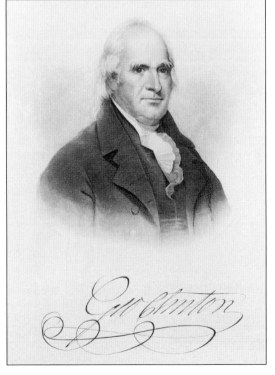

Flora Adams Darling helped found the Daughters of the American Revolution. When personal conflicts led to her split from the DAR, she founded the National Society of the US Daughters of 1812. In 1891, she organized the United Daughters of the Confederacy and became its director general. In later years, she was consumed by the idea that her daughter-in-law killed her son, a theory bolstered by the fact that the daughter-in-law then married her late husband's deathbed physician. Darling founded the Edward Irving Darling Musical Society in memory of her son, who was a composer, and wrote seven books, including *A Winning, Wayward Woman* and *Senator Athens, C.S.A* (Both, HCC.)

In 1795, before Washington was a city, a young Englishman named John Gadsby emigrated with his wife and family and opened a tavern in Alexandria, Virginia. Gadsby's tavern (still serving today) became a popular spot for the leaders of the new nation; nearly all the founding fathers dined and drank there at some point. In 1824, Gadsby bought the Franklin Hotel on Pennsylvania Avenue, which quickly became known as Gadsby's Hotel. However, the 40-minute carriage ride from Gadsby's to the Capitol made that location less than ideal. In 1826, he bought a row of houses at Sixth Street and Pennsylvania Avenue NW and turned them into one grand building. The result was the National Hotel, a grand and stylish destination for Washington's most fashionable visitors. Gadsby's family grew with his fortunes. In 1836, he purchased the Decatur House on Lafayette Square. When he died in 1844, at the age of 78, he had quite a fortune to pass on to his children and grandchildren. He is buried in the imposing Gadsby family vault along with his descendants. (HCC.)

Mary Claire Fuller was a Washington native who embarked upon a stage career as a teenager. Working with several different agencies, she starred in many one-reelers and short films, including the original *Frankenstein*. She starred in *What Happened to Mary?*—a film series that earned her a place as one of the silent screen's first superstars. She abruptly ended her film career after starring in *The Long Trail*. Cal York, in *Photoplay* magazine, asked: "Mary Fuller has disappeared. Her actor friends . . . have tried to find traces of her, without success . . . No doubt she prefers to remain in seclusion—but, why?" What was not publicly known was that her affair with a married man resulted in a nervous breakdown that necessitated a lengthy treatment. She later moved back to Washington to live with her mother. After her mother's death, her mental health deteriorated and she was confined in St. Elizabeths Hospital for 25 years until her death at age 85. No family could be located, her stardom had been forgotten, and the local papers carried no obituary. Her grave is unmarked. (HCC.)

When the Secret Service was first created in 1865, it agents (pictured below c. 1865) were tasked with investigating the counterfeiting of currency. The first director was William P. Wood, a Civil War "warden" of the prison in the Old Brick Capitol (now the location of the Supreme Court), which housed the likes of Confederate spy Rose Greenhow. Within a year of his appointment, the Secret Service had arrested over 200 counterfeiters. He resigned in 1869 amidst a scandal resulting from his failure to curtail a massive counterfeit US Treasury bond operation. Undeterred, he continued the pursuit of his nemesis, the counterfeiter William Brockway, who was finally brought to justice in 1870. The modern stone at Wood's gravesite was placed there in May 2001 by retired members of the Secret Service. (Above, HCC; below, LOC.)

Four

NOTABLE STONES
ANGELS, ARMOIRES, AND
LIBRARY CARDS

The gravestones in Congressional Cemetery tell their own stories. The colonial sandstone tablets give way to the ornate monuments and fancy flourishes of the Victorian era. Stones from the early 20th century have art nouveau details and stylized floral carvings. Contemporary stones come in shapes as varied as cubes and pyramids. Some are beautiful, others are poignant, and some are even whimsical. The most remarkable ones do not necessarily mark the graves of famous people. (HCC.)

Marion Ooletia Kahlert was just 10 years old when she died in 1904. Her striking statue became so popular with cemetery visitors that it was encased in protective glass for a time. That measure was not, as it turns out, overly cautious; the statue was vandalized later in the 20th century and subsequently removed from the cemetery grounds. The broken pieces await restoration in the cemetery offices. (HCC.)

In the midst of the Civil War, the arsenal in Washington was a major site of weapons manufacturing. On June 17, 1864, some ceramic shells that had been left in the sun to dry ignited. The arsenal exploded, killing 22 young women, most of whom were teenage Irish immigrants. Eighteen of the women were buried at Congressional Cemetery in a funeral procession led by Pres. Abraham Lincoln (the others were buried at Mount Olivet). Local sculptor Lot Flannery was commissioned to create this monument, which at a height of 25 feet is the tallest marker in the cemetery. It is topped by a statue of a downcast maiden. Images on the side include a winged hourglass and an engraving (now eroded) of the arsenal in flames. (LOC.)

An enormous totem dominates the southwest corner of the cemetery. Carved by members of the Lummi tribe of northwest Washington State, it was intended as a memorial to those killed at the Pentagon on September 11, 2001. It was installed at the Pentagon briefly, then moved to Congressional Cemetery. The left upright shows grandfather sun topped by father bear. The right upright shows grandmother moon (on the back of a turtle) and mother bear. The crossbar ends in two eagles. The eagle facing east, toward the rising sun, represents peace. The war eagle faces west and holds a man in its beak. The shape of the entire structure is meant to invoke a house, suggesting the togetherness of the "family" under the American roof. (LOC.)

On August 8, 1873, the steamboat *Wawaset*, a luxury ferry that carried passengers up and down the Chesapeake Bay, burst into flames within sight of the shore of the Potomac River at Chatterton's Landing in King George County, Virginia. Safety precautions were few; there were hundreds of life jackets on board and in easy reach, but there had never been any safety drills and no one thought to use them. The few that did survived. Passengers were burned, drowned, or crushed to death in the mad rush to escape, and over 80 people died. Six of them were members of the Reed family: 28-year-old Sarah Reed and her three children, cousin Bettie Reed, and her aunt Julia Kelly. (DCPL.)

Navy lieutenant John McLaughlin was only 36 when he died in 1847, but he must have gained quite a reputation in his short life. His extraordinary monument, in the shape of an upended cannon, bears several inscriptions on its base. One reads, "The trust committed to him shows the appreciation of his government, this marble the estimation of his friends." (HCC.)

Sally Wood Nixon was an active member of the Daughters of the American Revolution and the Colonial Dames of America. When she died in 1937, she was memorialized with a stone modeled after her favorite piece of furniture. The Art Deco housing is carved from granite, and the doors are glass-fronted with a metal grille that has oxidized to a bluish green. The locked doors of the armoire open, revealing an urn that contains Nixon's remains. (HCC.)

Maria Estelle Kretschmar died of diphtheria just shy of her ninth birthday in 1885. Her grave, very popular with photographers, is marked with a pretty marble statue of a little girl with ringlets who is bunching up her skirt. Visitors often leave coins in her skirt, which are regularly collected and added to the cemetery's donation jar. (Both, HCC.)

The grave of Catherine Weller is a grand example of late-18th-century statuary. The heroic figure with a flowing cape clings to a cross. It may have been a stock figure offered by the stonemason—perhaps the "faith" figure in a trio of faith, hope, and charity. If so, it is the only example of that figure in Congressional Cemetery. Other stock figures are repeated on more than one grave. Unfortunately, the structure of this statue did not stand the test of time; more than 100 years after Weller's death, her monument is missing its forearms and the top of its cross. (Both, HCC.)

When the fraternal society Woodmen of the World was founded in 1890, they developed the motto "no Woodmen shall rest in an unmarked grave." Early members received a free monument from the society. Gravestones were originally intended to be a uniform design sent by the home office to local stonecutters, but not all the cutters followed the design. Some used their own interpretation of the Woodmen design, which they felt was more appropriate. A tree stump—part of the society's logo—is the most common symbol used on gravestone designs. Congressional Cemetery includes several Woodmen monuments, all slightly different. The tradition was discontinued in the 1920s when cemeteries began prohibiting aboveground markers, which increased the cost of maintenance. (HCC.)

The use of angels in funerary art is as old as Christian art itself. At Congressional Cemetery, there are many beautiful examples of angelic statuary from the 19th and 20th centuries—some towering and inspiring, others small and heartwarming. The smaller versions, sometimes referred to as cherubs, tend to watch over children that passed away, and the angels standing eternally above their resting places serve as protection and comfort. Adults, however (especially powerful and/or wealthy ones), preferred that their earthly remains and soul be protected by a full-grown angel, emanating strength and perpetuity. (Both, HCC.)

The angel that stands over the tomb of Choctaw chief Peter Pitchlynn is holding a writing implement, alluding that perhaps the pen is indeed mightier than the sword. (HCC.)

In the case of the archangel that watches over the mother of Mary Ann Hall, her torch is aloft, leading the deceased toward eternal reward and redemption. The faded scarf wrapped around the archangel's neck is the source of a cemetery ghost story; legend has it that if the scarf is removed, it will reappear within 24 hours by the spirit of the benevolent Mary, forever watching out for her mother. (HCC.)

This monument is not stone—it is one of a half-dozen "zinkers" at Congressional Cemetery. Beginning in 1874, the Monumental Bronze Company molded pure zinc into elegant, personalized, and inexpensive cemetery memorials, available to the public through mail order catalogs. A simple plaque with the details of the deceased could be screwed into place by the customer. The concept was novel, as were the monuments themselves. Zinc, a nonmagnetic metal roughly the same weight as iron, develops a protective coating of zinc carbonate and zinc oxide when exposed to the air. The coating is usually dark gray, but the Monumental Bronze Company sandblasted their products. This technique lightened the patina to the distinctive blue-gray these "zinkers" are known for. (HCC.)

This pyramid-shaped monument was erected in memory of Frederick Rodgers, who drowned at age 17 while serving in the Navy. The inscription notes that "this tomb was raised by his Father," John Rodgers, who died 10 years later as "a senior officer of the United States Navy, after forty one years of brilliant and important service." As with other early monuments at Congressional, the pyramid is made of sandstone. Its distinctive shape was included in Victorian postcards featuring cemetery views like the one shown below. (Right, HCC; below, DCPL.)

BURIAL GROUND

(Congressional)

The obelisk can be traced back to ancient Egypt, where it first symbolized the arms of Ra, the sun god. The obelisk represented a sort of petrified ray reaching up to the sky, perforating the clouds and breaking up negative energy. The obelisk eventually became an iconic symbol of power and protection. The towering figure of the obelisk worked its way into Western culture as a novelty of Egypt's impressive past. Other than the traditional tablet, the obelisk is the most common form of monument in Congressional Cemetery. (Both, HCC.)

During the Victorian age, use of the obelisk came into vogue because many non-Catholic churchyards felt that the cross was "too Catholic" and so began using classical, non-Christian imagery on grave sites. The use of such symbolism continues today, though the impetus may be different. The symbolic representation of protection provided by the obelisk has endured through the ages. At Congressional Cemetery, a stroll around the grounds will demonstrate that in every decade of the past two centuries the obelisk has been (and still is) a venerated marker for a departed loved one's grave. (Both, HCC.)

Taza (Tahzay) was a son of the great Cochise, the Apache chief known for his ability to keep peace among warring factions of the Apache Nation. Taza became the leader of his father's followers when Cochise died in 1874. Taza strove to honor his father's legacy, but he could not unite the various Apache bands as Cochise had done. In the summer of 1876, Taza joined an Apache delegation travelling to the East Coast to perform Indian dances at the American centennial. During this trip, Taza succumbed to pneumonia and was buried in the Congressional Cemetery. His stone, which was installed by the American Indian Society of Washington, DC, in 1971, was based on this photograph from the Library of Congress collection—although it is now believed to be a portrait of his cousin. (Above, HCC; left, LOC.)

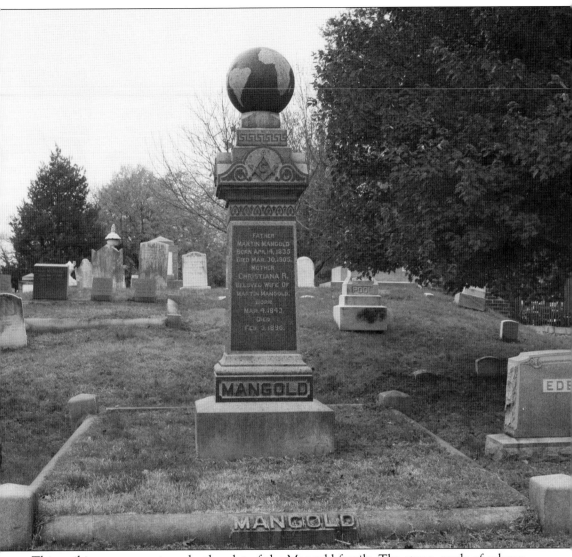

This striking monument marks the plot of the Mangold family. The stone, made of solemn gray granite, stands over several generations of Mangolds, who were local residents of Capitol Hill. The traditional column includes many symbols, including the Masonic protractor and the Greek key motif. The monument is topped by a geographically accurate planet Earth, with the oceans fashioned out of polished granite and the continents left with a matte finish. Over 100 years after its installation, the stone still looks new, in striking contrast to the weathered marble monuments nearby. (HCC.)

Downcast maidens can be found on gravestones throughout Congressional Cemetery. Maiden statues weep over the graves of males and females both young and old. They often include other symbols of purity and grief, such as lilies of the valley or drooping rosebuds. (Both, HCC.)

Some of the statues are custom-built; others are stock figures. Over time, even similar statues weather differently, so the face of each maiden seems to have its own singular expression. Some seem tragic, others serene, and some have faces hidden from view. (Both, HCC.)

WILLIAM HENRY HILL
1813 — 1858
HIS WIFE
ALICE DREW HILL
1818 — 1900
LYDIA ELIZABETH HILL

Many monuments include icons of religious faith, such as crosses, symbols of the spirit (flame or butterfly), symbols of Christ (dove or lamb), and initials such as "IHS" or "XP" as shorthand for Christ. The Coyle monument includes a crown, representing the majesty of God and Christ in the Kingdom of Heaven. The inscription under the Bible reads, "Ye shall receive a crown of glory that fadeth not away." (HCC.)

Through much of its early history, the cemetery served as both a public park and a burial ground. Families came for the day, and gravestones in the form of tables were used for picnics. A contemporary monument expands on the concept and is designed as a perfect picnic site, complete with benches and a shady weeping willow. When commissioned, it was hoped that the monument would provide a place for visitors to enjoy for hundreds of years to come. (HCC.)

Unfortunately, the original table-top tombstones were fashioned of marble or weaker stone than the granite used in the monument described above. Many have deteriorated over time. A few have collapsed from the weight of the water that collects in the bowed midsections of the tables. (HCC.)

Visitors regularly worry that the upended cube is tipping over, but it was designed to stand on one corner. The couple buried underneath were artists and teachers; perhaps they wanted cemetery visitors to look at their surroundings from a new perspective. (HCC.)

Just as the simple tablets of the early 1800s gave way to elaborate Victorian monuments, imaginative modern stones are replacing the uniform granite markers of the 20th century. This pink granite pyramid is carved with epitaphs on all four sides. One says, "Only those things spiritual are eternal—truth, justice, love, mercy, and liberty." (HCC.)

Ruth Ann Overbeck was a historian and librarian who knew the value of research. Instead of including her personal data on her stone, she challenges the visitor to "Look it up!" (HCC.)

Older stones have traditional epitaphs or Bible verses carved upon them; some of the contemporary stones are less predictable. Photojournalist Jeffrey Heiners's stone looks conservative from the front, but the back is carved with "Mistah Heinah he no home!"—something the deceased apparently said to unwanted callers. (HCC.)

Mann, Thomas, 1948-
    Librarian. Chicago: Charles H. and Margaret Mann,
1948.

    Rev. ed. Baton Rouge, 1976; Washington, DC, 1980.
    Future corrected edition in the hands of a Higher Editor.

    I. Christian. I.

Z710.M23   025.5 24   0221-1948
                        AACR2 MARC

Library of Congress

More than one stone in the cemetery has been designed by a living person for him or herself, then installed and ready to be engraved with a date of death. Thomas Mann, a librarian at the Library of Congress, created a stone that looks like a card from a library's card catalog, complete with a hole at the bottom for a steel rod. There is a divot on top for visitors to leave a coin, which Mann insists brings good luck to librarians. The data entries and Dewey Decimal codes refer to places Mann has lived and books he has published. The stone includes an epitaph that reads, "Future corrected edition in the hands of a Higher Editor." (HCC.)

Five

FAVORITE STORIES
ODDBALLS, SCOUNDRELS,
AND UNSUNG HEROES

There are 55,000 people buried in Congressional Cemetery, but there are only about 14,000 stones. Some tombstones document multiple interments at the same site. Other sites were never marked by families who could not afford the cost of a tombstone. In addition, many stones have collapsed and been buried. Whether or not a tombstone exists, newspapers document the fascinating stories behind the stones. (HCC.)

Stephen Pleasonton was a clerk in the Treasury Department during the War of 1812. Upon hearing rumors that the British were nearby, he and others obtained course linen bags into which they placed the original Declaration of Independence, the Articles of Confederation, most of the international treaties and national laws, and Gen. George Washington's Revolutionary War papers, together with many other documents. Despite the great demand for wagons or anything with wheels, Pleasonton found some carts and, amid the general panic, carted the bags to a mill beyond Georgetown. In the middle of the night, he decided this location lacked security and decided to take the documents by horseback to Leesburg, 35 miles away. (Left, LOC; below, HCC.)

Stephen Pleasonton had interesting children, too, who are now buried in front of their parents. Stephen Pleasonton's most notable son was Gen. Alfred Pleasonton, a cavalry officer who saw battle at Antietam and Chancellorsville during the Civil War. He resigned his commission in 1868 and later worked for the predecessor of the Internal Revenue Service, but he was dismissed for lobbying Congress to repeal the federal income tax. Gen. Augustus Pleasonton served as commander of the home guard of Philadelphia during the Civil War, but he was better known as the originator of the theory that the sun's rays, when passed through blue glass, were particularly stimulating not only to vegetation, but to the health and growth of animals. The theory attracted widespread attention and engendered the "blue-glass craze" of the 1870s. (HCC.)

THE LADY FRANKLIN BAY ARCTIC EXPEDITION

Seated (left to right): Private Maurice Connell, Sergeant David L. Brainard, Lieutenant Frederick F. Kislingbury, Lieutenant Adolphus W. Greely, Lieutenant James B. Lockwood, Sergeant Edward Israel, Sergeant Winfield S. Jewell, Sergeant George W. Rice

Standing: Private William Whisler, Private William A. Ellis, Private Jacob Bender, Sergeant William H. Cross, Private Julius Fredericks, Sergeant David Linn, Private Henry Biederbick, Private Charles B. Henry, Private Francis Long, Sergeant David C. Ralston, Corporal Nicholas Salor, Sergeant Hampden S. Gardiner, Corporal Joseph Elison. Dr. Octave Pavy, who joined the expedition in Greenland, is missing from the group.

Sgt. William H. Cross (standing, fourth from left) was a member of the Lady Franklin Bay Arctic expedition, better known as the Greely Expedition. The goal of the expedition was to collect scientific data from the high Arctic. From the beginning, the expedition was plagued by bad luck, bad weather, and bad management. Cross was the first member of the party to succumb to starvation and exposure near Cape Sabine. Eventually, 19 of the 25 men perished, and the *New York Times* suggested that survivors resorted to cannabalism. Currently no evidence has been found to confirm or refute the claim. (Above, HCC; below, LOC.)

Left almost totally deaf by a childhood illness, Fielding Bradford Meek taught himself about the world around him. By 1857, the Smithsonian Institution was building a reputation among natural scientists, and Meek decided it was the perfect place for a paleontologist like himself. He and other bachelor scientists lived at the brand new Smithsonian Castle. The Castle scientists formed a group called the "Megatherium Club," named after an extinct species of giant sloth. They built trapdoors between their rooms, they held sack races in the Castle's Great Hall, and they serenaded the daughters of the Smithsonian's secretary. In 1876, just after his 59th birthday, Meek died of tuberculosis. His funeral was held in the Castle. His gravestone reads, "Fielding Bradford Meek, Paleontologist," and features a pick and a quill, the tools of his trade. (Above left, LOC; above right, HCC; below right, HCC.)

In the early 1900s, the game of baseball was not for the faint of heart. Infielders routinely earned bloody gashes from the spikes of sliding runners. Runners regularly took elbows to the ribs or sharp kicks to the shins from basemen. Outfielders played drunk, pitchers threw spitballs, and spectators tossed beer bottles at the umpires. To survive in the so-called "deadball era," a player had to be fierce, sneaky, and a little bit nutty. Fortunately, Art Devlin was all three. In her history of the 1908 World Series, journalist Cait Murphy says, "Devlin fits the stereotype of a ballplayer, being feisty and Irish." Devlin was not afraid to play dirty. Many an opposing player was thrown out at home after being slowed down by a vicious bounce from Devlin's broad shoulders as the unsuspecting runner rounded third. (Both, HCC.)

ARTHUR DEVLIN

Arthur Devlin joined the Giants in 1904, and has since been a mainstay of the team, doing grand work and plenty of it. Although he led the third basemen in 1908, it was not because he dodged the difficult fielding chances and thus escaped errors. On the contrary, he had a total for 1908, 1909 and 1910 of 573 put outs and 932 assists, more than any other third baseman in the National League, and some of his stops looked impossible before he made them.

	G.	B.	F.
1908	157	.253	.947
1909	143	.265	.934
1910	147	.260	.933

BASE BALL SERIES
ASSORTED DESIGNS
POLAR BEAR
ALWAYS THE BEST.
FACTORY No 6 1ST DIST. O.

James Croggon was a native Washingtonian who covered his hometown for local newspapers for over 50 years. As a young man, he covered the Lincoln assassination and subsequent trials for the *Evening Star*, where he remained a daily reporter until 1894. Croggon was covering Pres. James Garfield's appearance at the old Pennsylvania Railroad station when Garfield was shot. Croggon's article is considered one of the best eyewitness accounts of the assassination. After retiring from daily deadlines, Croggon wrote special features for the *Star*, including a series called "Old Washington" that contained nostalgic stories of the capital of Croggon's youth. (HCC.)

Emerick Hansell was a State Department courier who was in the wrong place at the wrong time. On April 14, 1865, Hansell was assigned to bring some papers to the home of Secretary of State William Seward, who was bedridden at home after a carriage accident. Hansell was there when Lewis Powell (also known as Payne, pictured below), one of John Wilkes Booth's coconspirators, arrived to assassinate Seward. When the servant would not let him in, Powell knocked him down, charged up the stairs, clobbered one of Seward's sons with his pistol, stabbed the other son, stabbed the Army nurse at Seward's bedside, and slashed Seward so viciously that his whole cheek flapped away from his skull. Then, on his way down the stairs, Powell slashed Hansell and fled. Amazingly, all survived the attack. The story of the Lincoln assassination is retold periodically at Congressional Cemetery, with actors portraying the eyewitnesses. (Left, HCC; below, LOC.)

John Payne Todd was Dolley Madison's son from her first marriage. Todd's father and brother died from yellow fever when he was an infant, and he was adopted by his stepfather James Madison when he was only two. Todd was a classic ne'er-do-well—in and out of debtor's prison, drinking, gambling, and breaking his mother's heart. Todd is largely responsible for the massive debt his mother accrued after President Madison's death and part of the reason she did not have a proper burial until years after her death (see page 32). History remembers Todd as a man highly beloved by his doting mother—and hardly anyone else. (Right, HCC; below, LOC.)

Nellie H. Bradley was a temperance activist. Under the pen name "Stella of Washington," she wrote stirring temperance anthems like "Father's a Drunkard and Mother is Dead," and "Marry No Man if He Drinks." Bradley also wrote plays and poems focused on the temperance message, with names like *The First Glass; or, the Power of Woman's Influence* and *The Young Teetotaler, or, Saved at Last.* Bradley is buried in the plot of the Brisseys, the family of her sister's husband. (Both, HCC.)

Scarlet Crow (more correctly translated Scarlet Raven), or Kangi Duta, was a member of the Sisseton Wahpeton Sioux tribe who came to Washington in 1867 to seek justice from the federal government. Scarlet Raven had served as a scout for the US Army during the Dakota (Sioux) Uprising of 1862 and objected to the removal of his tribe from Minnesota to South Dakota. A few days before the final negotiations, Scarlet Raven was reported missing, and the treaty was signed without him. His death was ruled a suicide, but the circumstances remain suspicious. Neither the rope nor the tree branch he was meant to have used to hang himself would have supported the weight of anyone larger than a child. Despite evidence of foul play, the death was never investigated. (Right, HCC; below, LOC.)

Count Adam de Gurowski was a Polish intellectual of uncertain origin. He came to America in 1849, saying he had been kicked out of Eastern Europe for his revolutionary views. He spent the Civil War years in Washington, by most accounts alienating the locals. Eccentrically dressed in a long flowing coat and colored glasses and known for his unpredictable temper, he is said to be the only man President Lincoln truly feared. Julia Ward Howe called de Gurowski a remarkable character, in whom "generous impulses warred with an undisciplined temper." His social sponsor in Civil War Washington was Fanny Eames, who stuck to de Gurowski long after others had given him up. He is buried in the Eames family plot—between Fanny and her husband. (HCC.)

Albert Ports (right) was employed as a "rigger" at the Capitol, where it was his job to keep the massive Statue of Freedom clean and swap out her lightning rods on a regular basis. Known as "The Human Fly" for his agility and complete lack of fear, Ports designed and installed scaffolding around the statue the first time he climbed up to give her a bath. In an interview with Capitol historian Smith Fry, Ports said, "There is only a four-inch surface on which to construct a rigging around the Goddess, and it is ticklish work. But I have never been dizzy in my life, and I had an exhilarating experience making the rigging. I can go up there in my stocking feet and climb to the top of the head of the goddess, just by clinging to her bronze robes. Of course, if I'd slip, there'd be a funeral, and there would be lots of nice things said in print about old Al that are not being said about him while he hustles around this big building." Ports died a natural death in 1910; his grave is unmarked. (LOC.)

Andrew Humphreys (left) commanded Union troops at Antietam and Fredericksburg. By the Battle at Gettysburg, he had command of a division in the III Corps and five days later was named Gen. George G. Meade's chief of staff. Later that year, he took command of the II Corps and was breveted to major general. Andrew's younger brother Joseph Humphreys married a woman from Virginia. When the war broke out, he joined the Confederate Navy, possibly choosing that side of the war because of his business and marriage ties. (LOC.)

Any ideological differences the brothers may have held in life are absent in death, as they were buried close to each other, although it is clear from the relative size and grandeur of their monuments which side was victorious. (Both, HCC.)

This impressive stone marks the grave of Alexander Dallas Bache, superintendent of the US Coast Survey. Descended from a long line of prominent politicians (his uncle was Vice Pres. George Dallas; his great-grandfather was Benjamin Franklin), Bache was an engineering professor at West Point (from which he graduated first in the class of 1825) and the University of Pennsylvania early in his career. As superintendent of the US Coast Survey, Bache was responsible for producing accurate charts of the coastlines of the entire United States. (Above, HCC; right, LOC.)

"BEAU" HICKMAN

Robert "Beau" Hickman was a charming scoundrel who boasted he had never worked a day in his life. He cut a dashing figure in Washington society with his tall beaver hat, diamond stickpin, and silver-handled cane. After quickly blowing through a small inheritance, Hickman lived off the generosity of others, actually receiving an allowance from some of his more prominent admirers. Despite his broad social circle, Hickman died penniless and was buried in a pauper's grave. When his old drinking buddies learned of his uncelebrated death, they decided to give Hickman a proper burial. They arrived at potter's field, interrupted body snatchers at Hickman's grave, and drove his remains to Congressional, where they arranged for a gravesite and stone. Hickman's ghost, complete with hat and stickpin, is said to haunt the site of the old National Hotel, where he and his friends enjoyed themselves at the bar in life. (Above, DCPL; left, HCC.)

George Watterston served as the first full-time librarian of Congress, from 1815 to 1829. Before Watterson's term, the clerk of the House of Representatives was responsible for maintaining the library. When the library was burned in 1814 during the War if 1812, the job of librarian became a separate position. Watterston replenished the library by purchasing the collection of former president Thomas Jefferson and organizing it based on Jefferson's classification scheme. After opposing Andrew Jackson's campaign for president, Watterston was fired by Jackson in 1829. Watterston spent the remainder of his life trying to get his job back. He is buried in the Watterston family vault, one of several brick-and-mortar crypts on the cemetery grounds. (Right, HCC; below, LOC.)

Sen. Andrew Pickens Butler of South Carolina coauthored the Kansas-Nebraska Act of 1854, which many abolitionists thought undermined the Missouri Compromise of 1820. In 1856, Sen. Charles Sumner of Massachusetts gave a speech denigrating Butler, even mocking his speech impediment that was caused by a medical condition. Two days later, Butler's nephew, Rep. Preston Brooks of South Carolina (whose cenotaph is about 100 feet away from his uncle's) defended the family honor. He beat Sumner with a cane on the floor of the Senate as a colleague brandishing a pistol held at bay anyone coming to Sumner's aid. Sumner did not return to the Senate for three years, standing for reelection while convalescing. The attack galvanized both sides of the debate and transformed the struggling Republican Party into a political force. (Above, HCC; below, LOC.)

AWFUL EXPLOSION OF THE *"PEACE-MAKER"* ON BOARD THE U.S. STEAM FRIGATE, *PRINCETON*, ON WEDNESDAY, 28TH FEB: 1844.

In which melancholy accident, the Sec.ed of State M.r Upshur, the Sec.y of the Navy M.r Gilmer, Com.r Kennon, M.r Gardiner of N.Y. & M.r Maxcy were instantly killed.....Capt. Stockton & C.e of the Ships Company wounded.

On February 29, 1844, a report in the *National Intelligencer* stated: "In the whole course of our lives it has never fallen to our lot to announce to our readers a more shocking calamity—shocking in all its circumstances and concomitants—than that which occurred on board the United States Ship *Princeton*, yesterday afternoon, whilst under way, in the river Potomac, fourteen or fifteen miles below this city." Four hundred guests, including Pres. John Tyler, had sailed on the USS *Princeton* for an exhibition of the ship's impressive weaponry. One of the guns exploded, killing eight guests, including Secretary of State Abel Upshur and Capt. Beverly Kennon, who was chief of the Bureau of Construction, Equipment, and Repairs. Both were buried under this sandstone monument, although both were reinterred 30 years later in the Upshur plot in Oak Hill Cemetery. (Above, LOC; right, HCC.)

Adm. French Forrest served in the War of 1812 and the Mexican War. He commanded the Washington Navy Yard from 1855 to 1856. In April 1861, he resigned his Navy commission and, days later, joined the Confederate Navy from Virginia. As the third-highest-ranking officer in the Navy, he commanded the Norfolk Navy Yard and refit the USS *Merrimack* into the ironclad CSS *Virginia*. He watched the Battle of Hampton Roads from a tug in the harbor in March 1862. When Norfolk fell two months later, he transferred to Richmond and was off the rolls of the Confederate Navy by mid-1864. Buried next to Forrest is his wife, Emily, whose stone, curiously enough, does not say she died, but rather that she "translated" in 1880. (Left, HCC; below, LOC.)

COL. JOHN W. SIMONTON,
OF KEYWEST FLORIDA.
DIED MAY 1854. AGED 63 YR'S.
HIS WIFE
ANN SIMONTON,
DIED JULY 3, 1834. AGED 29 YR'S
THEIR DAUGHTER
FLORIDA.
FEB. 9, 1830. AUG. 13, 1878.

John W. Simonton's gravestone reads, "Of Keywest Florida," but that appellation was once far from being written in stone. Simonton purchased the island that became known as Key West in 1822. Unfortunately, someone else had bought the island, too—the original owner sold it twice. To make matters more complicated, the new, competing owner had also sold the island twice. After a complex legal battle, Simonton was declared the rightful owner, and the town of Key West was incorporated in 1828 in the territory of Florida. Buried in the same plot are Simonton's wife, Ann, and their daughter, whose name, appropriately enough, was Florida. (HCC.)

Pringle and Robert Slight were father-and-son carpenters who both worked at the Capitol. Pringle was an all-around handyman, unclogging gutters and fixing stuck desk drawers. When the original Capitol dome was replaced by the taller version, it was Pringle who figured out how to dismantle the old one. Robert was working on the new dome when he fell from the scaffolding, eventually dying as a result of his injuries. Some say they have seen Robert Slight's ghost floating around the Capitol dome, a tray of carpenter's tools in his hand. (Left, HCC; below, LOC.)

Clyde Tolson was associate director of the FBI in charge of personnel. Although he had been a gun-slinging agent early in his career, a 1964 stroke left him in frail health. Tolson was probably best known as the best friend of J. Edgar Hoover (see page 40). When Hoover died in 1972, Tolson, Hoover's sole heir, bought the nearest available gravesite to the Hoover family plot. Tolson died in 1975. (HCC.)

In addition to Pres. Abraham Lincoln's valet Charles Forbes (see page 60) and accidental stabbing victim Emerick Hansell (see page 108), there are many people buried at Congressional Cemetery who have some connection to the assassination of Lincoln. Margaret and Cranston Laurie and their daughter Belle Youngs were popular mediums in Civil War–era Washington. Mary Todd Lincoln regularly invited them to the White House for séances. As depicted in this engraving, the president even participated once or twice and was present on the occasion that Youngs reportedly levitated a grand piano. (HCC.)

Peter Taltavull was the owner and bartender at the Star Saloon, which was located next door to Ford's Theatre. John Wilkes Booth hung out at the Star while waiting for the right moment to run to the theater and shoot President Lincoln. Booth, an actor, knew the play *Our American Cousin* very well and was waiting for a big laugh late in the second act that would cover the sound of the gunshot. (HCC.)

James Pumphrey ran a livery business near Ford's Theatre. On the morning of the assassination, Booth, a regular customer, came in to rent a horse. His regular horse was not available, so Pumphrey gave him a spirited mare. He also lent Booth spurs to help keep the mare in line. After Booth shot Lincoln, he jumped down to the stage, supposedly snagging the spurs on the bunting and breaking his leg. (HCC.)

John Buckingham was the doorkeeper at Ford's Theatre. Between drinks at the Star Saloon, Booth would run into the theater lobby and ask Buckingham the time. Immediately after the shooting, Buckingham and others who were about the theater were rounded up, taken to the Navy Yard, and confined until the preliminary investigation into the murder had been concluded. Buckingham was released a few days later. (HCC.)

INDEX

About the APHCC

The Association for the Preservation of Historic Congressional Cemetery (APHCC) is a nonprofit organization that manages the cemetery on behalf of Christ Church, Washington Parish. The mission of the APHCC is to serve the community as an active burial ground and conserve the physical artifacts, buildings, and infrastructure of the cemetery; to celebrate the American heritage represented by those interred there; restore and sustain the landscape; to protect the Anacostia River watershed; and to manage the grounds as an accessible community resource. More information can be found at www.congressionalcemetery.org.

DISCOVER THOUSANDS OF LOCAL HISTORY BOOKS
FEATURING MILLIONS OF VINTAGE IMAGES

Arcadia Publishing, the leading local history publisher in the United States, is committed to making history accessible and meaningful through publishing books that celebrate and preserve the heritage of America's people and places.

Find more books like this at
www.arcadiapublishing.com

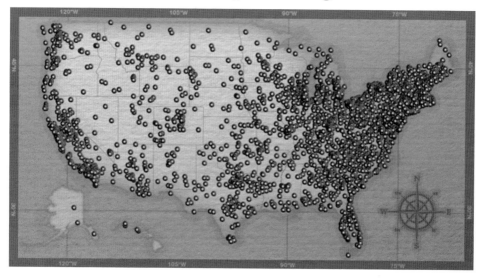

Search for your hometown history, your old stomping grounds, and even your favorite sports team.

Consistent with our mission to preserve history on a local level, this book was printed in South Carolina on American-made paper and manufactured entirely in the United States. Products carrying the accredited Forest Stewardship Council (FSC) label are printed on 100 percent FSC-certified paper.

MADE IN THE USA